1000 German words

compiled by John Williams BA (Hons)

Published in Great Britain by World International Publishing Limited,
an Egmont Company, Egmont House,
PO Box III, Great Ducie Street,
Manchester M60 3BL.

Printed in Finland.
ISBN 0 7498 1436 5

A catalogue record for this book is available from the British Library.

contents

notes to readers

This book contains many of the most useful words you will need to know when you start learning German. However, on its own, it will not tell you how to speak or write correct German sentences. For that you will need a proper textbook, and probably a good teacher as well!

nouns and gender

There are two very important features of German that you will need to know about right from the start. Firstly, every **noun** (a word which means a thing, a person or an idea) begins with a capital letter. Secondly, every noun belongs to one of three different types, or **genders**. These genders are called **masculine**, **feminine** and **neuter**. It is as if everything in the world was either 'he' (masculine), 'she' (feminine) or 'it' (neuter). The idea of genders might seem rather strange when you are talking about objects. For instance, a skirt is masculine, a boy's trousers are feminine, and a girl is neuter!

In this book we have tried to help you learn genders by showing each German noun, wherever we can, together with its word for 'the', which changes according to whether the noun is masculine or feminine.

With singular masculine nouns, the word for 'the' is **der**, with feminine nouns it is **die**, and with neuter nouns it is **das**. So, whenever you learn a new noun you should also learn whether it takes **der**, **die** or **das**.

With a few nouns it is not possible to show the gender using these little words. In such cases we have shown the gender in brackets after the German word – **(m)** for masculine, **(f)** for feminine and **(n)** for neuter.

pronunciation

Under each German word we have shown its **pronunciation**, that is, the way it should be spoken. If you say these pronunciations as you would expect to say them in English, you will get quite close to the way the German words are actually spoken.

key to pronunciation

For longer words, the pronunciations are divided into **syllables**, to help you read and say them more easily. Usually, one syllable is written in heavier print than the others (**like this**). This means that this syllable should be said a little more loudly and strongly than the others.

( )	Letters in brackets are pronounced only slightly or not at all.
a	Sounds like the 'a' sound in 'cat' or 'and'.
ah	Sounds like the 'a' sound in 'father' or 'calm'.
ay	Sounds like the 'ay' sound in 'say' or 'able'.
e	Sounds like the 'e' sound in 'let' or 'end'.
e(r)	Sounds like the 'e' sound in 'the'.
g	Sounds like the 'g' sound in 'go' or 'big'.
i	Sounds like the 'i' sound in 'in' or 'sit'.
iy	Sounds like 'eye' or the 'i' sound in 'find'.
kh	Sounds like the 'ch' sound in the Scottish word 'loch'.
n(g)	Sounds like the 'ng' sound in 'singer' and 'song'. The 'g' is silent.
o	Sounds like the 'o' sound in 'hot' or 'odd'.
oh	Sounds like the 'o' sound in 'told' or 'rose'.
ow	Sounds like the 'ow' sound in 'how' or the 'ou' sound in 'out'.
s	Sounds like the 's' sound in 'say' or 'house'.
ts	Sounds like the 'ts' sound in 'cats' or the 'zz' sound in 'pizza'.
u	Sounds like the 'u' sound in 'put' or 'cushion'.
uh	Sounds like the 'ur' sound in 'fur', but the 'r' is silent.
yoo	Sounds like the 'ew' sound in 'new'.
(y)u	Sounds like the 'u' sound in 'June'.

umlauts

Some letters in German words have two dots (¨), known as an **umlaut**, above them. They change the way a particular letter is pronounced.

ä	The letter **ä** is pronounced **ay** or **e**.
äu	The letters **äu** are pronounced **oy**.
ö	The letter **ö** is pronounced **uh**.
ü	The letter **ü** is pronounced **(y)oo** or **(y)u**.

who are you?

address	die Adresse *dee a-**dre**-se(r)*
age	das Alter *das **al**-ter*
birthday	der Geburtstag *dair ge(r)-**boortz**-tahg*
boy	der Junge *dair **yun(g)**-e(r)*
child	das Kind *das kint*
girl	das Mädchen *das **mayt**-she(r)n*
I	ich *ikh*
my	mein *miyn*
name	der Name *dair **nah**-me(r)*
our	unser ***un**-zer*
we	wir *veer*
you	Sie *zee*
you *(to a friend)*	du *doo*
you *(to a group of friends)*	ihr *eer*
your	Ihr *eer*
your *(of a friend)*	dein *diyn*
your *(of a group of friends)*	euer ***oy**-er*

people

baby	**das Baby** *das **bay**-bee*
friend	**der Freund, die Freundin** *dair froynt, dee **froyn**-din*
gentleman	**der Herr** *dair hair*
he	**er** *air*
lady	**die Dame** *dee **dah**-me(r)*
man	**der Mann** *dair man*
Miss	**Fräulein** ***froy**-liyn*
Mr	**Herr** *hair*
Mrs	**Frau** *frow*
neighbour	**der Nachbar, die Nachbarin** *dair **nakh**-bah, dee **nakh**-ba-rin*
nobody	**niemand** ***nee**-mant*
people	**die Leute** *dee **loy**-te(r)*
person	**der Mensch** *dair mensh*
she	**sie** *zee*
somebody	**jemand** ***yay**-mant*
they	**sie** *zee*
woman	**die Frau** *dee frow*

the family

aunt

die Tante
*dee **tan**-te(r)*

brother

der Bruder
*dair **Broo**-der*

cousin

der Cousin, die Cousine
*dair koo-**za(n)**, dee koo-**zee**-ne(r)*

daughter

die Tochter
*dee **tokh**-ter*

family

die Familie
*dee fa-**mee**-lee-e(r)*

father

der Vater
*dair **fah**-ter*

grandfather

der Grossvater
*dair **grohs**-fah-ter*

grandmother

die Grossmutter
*dee **grohs**-mu-ter*

husband

der Mann
dair man

mother

die Mutter
*dee **mu**-ter*

nephew

der Neffe
*dair **ne**-fe(r)*

niece

die Nichte
*dee **nikh**-te(r)*

parents

die Eltern
*dee **el**-tairn*

sister

die Schwester
*dee **shwes**-ter*

son

der Sohn
dair zohn

uncle

der Onkel
*dair **on(g)**-ke(r)l*

wife

die Frau
dee frow

parts of the body

arm   der Arm
dair arm

back   der Rücken
*dair **r(y)u**-ke(r)n*

body   der Körper
*dair **kuhr**-per*

brain   das Gehirn
*das ge(r)-**heern***

chest   die Brust
dee brust

chin   das Kinn
das kin

ear   das Ohr
das ohr

elbow   der Ellbogen
*dair **el**-boh-ge(r)n*

eye   das Auge
*das **ow**-ge(r)*

eyebrow   die Augenbraue
*dee **ow**-ge(r)n-brow-e(r)*

face   das Gesicht
*das ge(r)-**zikht***

finger   der Finger
*dair **fin(g)**-e(r)*

foot   der Fuss
dair foos

forehead   die Stirn
dee shteern

hair   das Haar
das hahr

hand   die Hand
dee hant

head   der Kopf
dair kopf

heart	**das Herz** *das hairts*
knee	**das Knie** *das knee*
leg	**das Bein** *das biyn*
lip	**die Lippe** *dee li-pe(r)*
mouth	**der Mund** *dair munt*
nail	**der Nagel** *dair nah-ge(r)l*
neck	**der Hals** *dair hals*
nose	**die Nase** *dee nah-ze(r)*
shoulder	**die Schulter** *dee shul-ter*
skin	**die Haut** *dee howt*
stomach	**der Magen** *dair mah-ge(r)n*
thumb	**der Daumen** *dair dow-me(r)n*
toe	**die Zehe** *dee tsay-e(r)*
tongue	**die Zunge** *dee tsun(g)-e(r)*
tooth	**der Zahn** *dair tsahn*

clothes

belt	der Gürtel
	dair g(y)oor-te(r)l
blouse	die Bluse
	dee bloo-ze(r)
boot	der Stiefel
	dair shtee-fe(r)l
button	der Knopf
	dair knopf
cap	die Mütze
	dee m(y)oot-ze(r)
clothes	die Kleider
	dee kliy-der
coat	der Mantel
	dair man-te(r)l
dress	das Kleid
	das kliyt
to dress, to get dressed	sich an'ziehen
	zikh an-tsee-e(r)n
glove	der Handschuh
	dair hant-shoo
hat	der Hut
	dair hoot
jacket	die Jacke
	dee ya-ke(r)
knickers	das Höschen
	das huhz-she(r)n
pullover	der Pullover
	dair pu-loh-ver
to put on	an'ziehen
	an-tsee-e(r)n
raincoat	der Regenmantel
	dair ray-ge(r)n-man-te(r)l
scarf	das Halstuch
	das hals-tookh

shirt	**das Hemd** *das hemt*
shoe	**der Schuh** *dair shoo*
shorts	**die Shorts** *dee shorts*
skirt	**der Rock** *dair rok*
sleeve	**der Ärmel** *dair **air**-me(r)l*
sock	**die Socke** *dee **zo**-ke(r)*
sweatshirt	**das Sweatshirt** *das **swet**-shert*
to take off	**aus'ziehen** ***ows**-tsee-e(r)n*
tie	**die Krawatte** *dee kra-**va**-te(r)*
tights	**die Strumpfhose** *dee **shtrumpf**-hoh-ze(r)*
trousers	**die Hose** *dee **hoh**-ze(r)*
T-shirt	**das T-Shirt** *das **tee**-shert*
underpants	**die Unterhose** *dee **un**-ter-hoh-ze(r)*
to undress, to get undressed	**sich aus'ziehen** *zikh **ows**-tsee-e(r)n*
to wear	**tragen** ***trah**-ge(r)n*

the home

carpet	das Teppich *das **te**-pikh*
ceiling	die Decke *dee **de**-ke(r)*
chimney	der Schornstein *dair **shorn**-shtiyn*
curtain	der Vorhang *dair **for**-han(g)*
door	die Tür *dee t(y)oor*
doorbell	die Türklingel *dee **t(y)oor-**klin(g)-e(r)l*
downstairs	unten ***un**-te(r)n*
flat	die Wohnung *dee **voh**-nun(g)*
floor	der Fussboden *dair **foos**-boh-de(r)n*
house	das Haus *das hows*
key	der Schlüssel *dair **shl(y)u**-se(r)l*
to live	wohnen ***voh**-ne(r)n*
roof	das Dach *das dakh*
telephone	das Telefon *das tay-lay-**fohn***
upstairs	oben ***oh**-be(r)n*
wall	die Wand *dee vant*
window	das Fenster *das **fen**-ster*

rooms and furniture

a piece of furniture	das Möbel *das **muh**-be(r)l*
armchair	der Sessel *dair **ze**-se(r)l*
attic	der Dachboden *dair **dakh**-boh-de(r)n*
bathroom	das Badezimmer *das **bah**-de(r)-tsi-mer*
bedroom	das Schlafzimmer *das **shlahf**-tsi-mer*
chair	der Stuhl *dair shtool*
cupboard	der Schrank *dair shrank*
dining room	das Esszimmer *das **es**-tsi-mer*
kitchen	die Küche *dee **k(y)oo**-khe(r)*
living room	das Wohnzimmer *das **vohn**-tsi-mer*
room	das Zimmer *das **tsi**-mer*
settee, sofa	das Sofa *das **zoh**-fa*
shelf	das Brett *das bret*
table	der Tisch *dair tish*
toilet	die Toilette *dee toh-a-**le**-te(r)*
wardrobe	der Kleiderschrank *dair **kliy**-der-shrank*

in the bedroom

alarm clock	der Wecker *dair **ve**-ker*
bed	das Bett *das bet*
blanket	die Decke *dee **de**-ke(r)*
dream	der Traum *dair trowm*
to dream	träumen ***troy**-me(r)n*
dressing gown	der Bademantel *dair **bah**-de(r)-man-te(r)l*
duvet	die Steppdecke *dee **shtep**-de-ke(r)*
to get up	auf'stehen ***owf**-shtay-e(r)n*
lamp	die Lampe *dee **lam**-pe(r)*
nightie	das Nachthemd *das **nakht**-hemt*
pillow	das Kopfkissen *das **kopf**-ki-se(r)n*
pyjamas	der Schlafanzug *dair **shlahf**-an-tsoog*
sheet	das Bettlaken *das **bet**-lah-ke(r)n*
to sleep	schlafen ***shlah**-fe(r)n*
to go to sleep	ein'schlafen *i**yn**-shlah-fe(r)n*
slipper	der Pantoffel *dair pan-**to**-fe(r)l*
to wake up	auf'wachen ***owf**-va-khe(r)n*

in the bathroom

bath
(to have a bath)

das Bad
das baht

bath, bathtub

die Badewanne
*dee **bah**-de(r)-va-ne(r)*

comb

der Kamm
dair kam

to comb your hair

sich kämmen
*zikh **ke**-me(r)n*

flannel

der Waschlappen
*dair **vash**-la-pe(r)n*

mirror

der Spiegel
*dair **shpee**-ge(r)l*

shampoo

das Shampoo
*das sham-**poo***

shower

die Dusche
*dee **du**-she(r)*

soap

die Seife
*dee **ziy**-fe(r)*

sponge

der Schwamm
dair shwam

toilet

die Toilette
*dee toh-a-**le**-te(r)*

toilet paper

das Toilettenpapier
*das toh-a-**le**-te(r)n-pa-peer*

toothbrush

die Zahnbürste
*dee **tsahn**-b(y)oors-te(r)*

toothpaste

die Zahnpasta
*dee **tsahn**-pas-ta*

towel

das Handtuch
*das **hant**-tookh*

to wash

sich waschen
*zikh **va**-she(r)n*

washbasin

das Waschbecken
*das **vash**-be-ke(r)n*

eating and mealtimes

bowl	die Schüssel *dee **sh(y)u**-se(r)l*
breakfast	das Frühstück *das **fr(y)oo**-sht(y)uk*
cup	die Tasse *dee **ta**-se(r)*
dinner (in the evening)	das Abendessen *das **ah**-be(r)nt-e-se(r)n*
to drink	trinken ***trin(g)**-ke(r)n*
to eat	essen *e-se(r)n*
fork	die Gabel *dee **gah**-be(r)l*
glass	das Glas *das glahs*
hungry	hungrig ***hun(g)**-grig*
knife	das Messer *das **me**-ser*
lunch	das Mittagessen *das **mi**-tahg-e-se(r)n*
meal	die Mahlzeit *dee **mahl**-tsiyt*
plate	der Teller *dair **te**-ler*
saucer	die Untertasse *dee **un**-ter-ta-se(r)*
spoon	der Löffel *dair **luh**-fe(r)l*
supper (before bedtime)	der Imbiss *dair **im**-bis*
thirsty	durstig ***doors**-tig*

food and drink

biscuit — der Keks
dair kayks

bread — das Brot
das broht

butter — die Butter
*dee **bu**-ter*

cake — der Kuchen
*dair **koo**-khen*

cheese — der Käse
*dair **kay**-ze(r)*

chips — die Pommes frites
dee pom freets

chocolate — die Schokolade
*dee sho-ko-**lah**-de(r)*

coffee — der Kaffee
*dair ka-**fay***

cream — die Sahne
*dee **zah**-ne(r)*

crisps — die Chips
dee cheeps

egg — das Ei
das iy

flour — das Mehl
das mayl

food — das Essen
*das **e**-se(r)n*

ice cream — das Eis
das iys

jam — die Marmelade
*dee mar-me(r)-**lah**-de(r)*

juice — der Saft
dair zaft

lemonade — die Limonade
*dee li-mo-**nah**-de(r)*

margarine	**die Margarine** *dee mar-ga-**ree**-ne(r)*
milk	**die Milch** *dee milkh*
pepper	**der Pfeffer** *dair **pfe**-fer*
rice	**der Reis** *dair riys*
salad	**der Salat** *dair za-**laht***
salt	**das Salz** *das zalts*
soup	**die Suppe** *dee **zu**-pe(r)*
stew	**der Eintopf** *dair **iyn**-topf*
sugar	**der Zucker** *dair **tsu**-ker*
sweets	**die Bonbons** *dee bon(g)-**bon(g)z***
tea	**der Tee** *dair tay*
toast	**der Toast** *dair tohst*
vinegar	**der Essig** *dair **e**-sig*
water	**das Wasser** *das **va**-ser*
yoghurt	**der Joghurt** *dair **yoh**-goort*

vegetables

bean die Bohne
*dee **boh**-ne(r)*

cabbage der Kohl
dair kohl

carrot die Karotte
*dee ka-**ro**-te(r)*

cauliflower der Blumenkohl
*dair **bloo**-me(r)n-kohl*

celery die Stangensellerie
*dee **shtan(g)**-e(r)n-ze-le(r)-ree*

cucumber die Gurke
*dee **goor**-ke(r)*

onion die Zwiebel
*dee **tsvee**-be(r)l*

leek der Porree
*dair **po**-ray*

lettuce der Kopfsalat
*dair **kopf**-za-laht*

mushroom der Pilz
dair pilts

pea die Erbse
*dee **airp**-se(r)*

potato die Kartoffel
*dee kar-**to**-fe(r)l*

sprouts der Rosenkohl
*dair **roh**-ze(r)n-kohl*

sweetcorn der Mais
dair miys

tomato die Tomate
*dee to-**mah**-te(r)*

turnip die Rübe
*dee **r(y)oo**-be(r)*

vegetable das Gemüse
*das ge(r)-**m(y)oo**-ze(r)*

fruit

apple	der Apfel *dair **ap**-fe(r)l*
apricot	die Aprikose *dee a-pri-**koh**-ze(r)*
banana	die Banane *dee ba-**nah**-ne(r)*
blackcurrant	die schwarze Johannisbeere *dee **shwar**-tse(r) yo-**ha**-nis-bay-re(r)*
cherry	die Kirsche *dee **keer**-she(r)*
fruit	das Obst *das ohpst*
grape	die Traube *dee **trow**-be(r)*
grapefruit	die Grapefruit *dee **grayp**-froot*
lemon	die Zitrone *dee tsi-**troh**-ne(r)*
lime	die Limone *dee li-**moh**-ne(r)*
orange	die Orange *dee oh-**rah(n)**-zhe(r)*
peach	der Pfirsich *dair **pfeer**-zikh*
pear	die Birne *dee **beer**-ne(r)*
pineapple	die Ananas *dee **a**-na-nas*
plum	die Pflaume *dee **pflow**-me(r)*
raspberry	die Himbeere *dee **him**-bay-re(r)*
strawberry	die Erdbeere *dee **airt**-bay-re(r)*

meat and fish

bacon	der Speck *dair shpek*
beef	das Rindfleisch *das **rint**-fliysh*
chicken	das Hähnchen *das **hayn**-she(r)n*
chop	das Kotelett *das **koh**-te(r)-**let***
cod	der Kabeljau *dair **kah**-be(r)l-yow*
fish	der Fisch *dair fish*
fish finger	das Fischstäbchen *das **fish**-shtayb-she(r)n*
ham	der Schinken *dair **shin(g)**-ke(r)n*
hamburger	der Hamburger *dair **ham**-boor-ger*
lamb	das Lammfleisch *das **lam**-fliysh*
meat	das Fleisch *das fliysh*
pork	das Schweinefleisch *das **shwiy**-ne(r)-fliysh*
salmon	der Lachs *dair laks*
sausage	die Wurst *dee voorst*
steak	das Steak *das stayk*
tuna	der Thunfisch *dair **toon**-fish*
turkey	der Truthahn *dair **troot**-hahn*

in the kitchen

apron	die Schürze *dee **sh(y)oor**-tse(r)*
to cook	kochen ***ko**-khen*
cooker	der Herd *dair hairt*
dishcloth	der Spüllappen *dair **shp(y)ool**-la-pe(r)n*
dishwasher	die Geschirrspülmaschine *dee ge(r)-**sheer**-shp(y)ool-ma-shee-ne(r)*
to fry	braten ***brah**-te(r)n*
frying pan	die Bratpfanne *dee **braht**-pfa-ne(r)*
grill	der Grill *dair gril*
microwave	der Mikrowellenofen *dair **mee**-kro-ve-le(r)n-oh-fe(r)n*
oven	der Ofen *dair **oh**-fe(r)n*
pan	der Topf *dair topf*
sieve	das Sieb *das zeep*
sink	der Ausguss *dair **ows**-gus*
tap	der Hahn *dair hahn*
tea towel	das Geschirrtuch *das ge(r)-**sheer**-tookh*
to wash up	ab'waschen ***ap**-va-she(r)n*
washing machine	die Waschmaschine *dee **vash**-ma-shee-ne(r)*

in the garden

bush	der Busch *dair bush*
to dig	graben ***grah**-be(r)n*
flower	die Blume *dee **bloo**-me(r)*
garden	der Garten *dair **gar**-te(r)n*
gate	die Pforte *dee **pfor**-te(r)*
grass	das Gras *das grahs*
lawn	der Rasen *dair **rah**-ze(r)n*
lawnmower	der Rasenmäher *dair **rah**-ze(r)n-may-er*
leaf	das Blatt *das blat*
plant	die Pflanze *dee **pflan**-tse(r)*
soil	die Erde *dee **air**-de(r)*
spade	der Spaten *dair **shpah**-te(r)n*
tree	der Baum *dair bowm*
to water	sprengen ***shpren(g)**-e(r)n*
watering can	die Giesskanne *dee **gees**-ka-ne(r)*
weed	das Unkraut *das **un**-krowt*
wheelbarrow	die Schubkarre *dee **shoop**-ka-re(r)*

at school

| blackboard | die Tafel |
| | *dee **tah**-fe(r)l* |

| chalk | die Kreide |
| | *dee **kriy**-de(r)* |

| class | die Klasse |
| | *dee **kla**-se(r)* |

| classroom | das Klassenzimmer |
| | *das **kla**-se(r)n-tsi-mer* |

| desk | das Pult |
| | *das pult* |

| exam | die Prüfung |
| | *dee **pr(y)oo**-fun(g)* |

| head teacher | der Schulleiter, die Schulleiterin |
| | *dair **shool**-liy-ter, dee **shool**-liy-te(r)-rin* |

| to learn | lernen |
| | ***lair**-ne(r)n* |

| lesson | die Stunde |
| | *dee **shtun**-de(r)* |

| playground | der Schulhof |
| | *dair **shool**-hohf* |

| primary school | die Grundschule |
| | *dee **grunt**-shoo-le(r)* |

| pupil | der Schüler, die Schülerin |
| | *dair **sh(y)oo**-ler, dee **sh(y)oo**-le(r)-rin* |

| school | die Schule |
| | *dee **shoo**-le(r)* |

| secondary school | die Realschule |
| | *dee re-**ahl**-shoo-le(r)* |

| to teach | unterrichten |
| | *un-ter-**rikh**-te(r)n* |

| teacher | der Lehrer, die Lehrerin |
| | *dair **lay**-rer, dee **lay**-re(r)-rin* |

| test | die Klassenarbeit |
| | *dee **kla**-se(r)n-ar-biyt* |

school subjects

arithmetic	das Rechnen *das **rekh**-ne(r)n*
art	die Kunst *dee kunst*
chemistry	die Chemie *dee khay-**mee***
English	Englisch (n) ***en(g)**-glish*
French	Französisch (n) *fran-**tsuh**-zish*
games	der Sport *dair shport*
geography	die Geographie *dee ge-o-gra-**fee***
German	Deutsch (n) *doytsh*
history	die Geschichte *dee ge(r)-**shikh**-te(r)*
mathematics	die Mathematik *dee ma-te-ma-**teek***
music	die Musik *dee mu-**zeek***
nature study	die Naturkunde *dee na-**toor**-kun-de(r)*
physical education	das Turnen *das **toor**-ne(r)n*
physics	die Physik *dee f(y)oo-**zeek***
religious education	die Religion *dee re-li-gi-**ohn***
science	die Naturwissenschaft *dee na-**toor**-vi-se(r)n-shaft*
subject	das Fach *das fakh*

reading, writing and drawing

alphabet	**das Alphabet** *das al-fa-**bayt***
book	**das Buch** *das bookh*
capital letter	**der Grossbuchstabe** *dair **grohs**-bookh-shtah-be(r)*
comic	**der Comic** *dair **ko**-mik*
comma	**das Komma** *das **ko**-ma*
to copy	**kopieren** *ko-**peer**-e(r)n*
crayon	**der Buntstift** *dair **bunt**-shtift*
to draw	**zeichnen** ***tsiykh**-ne(r)n*
envelope	**der Umschlag** *dair **um**-shlahg*
exercise book	**das Heft** *das heft*
full stop	**der Punkt** *dair punkt*
letter *(that you send)*	**der Brief** *dair breef*
line	**die Zeile** *dee **tsiy**-le(r)*
magazine	**die Zeitschrift** *dee **tsiyt**-shrift*
newspaper	**die Zeitung** *dee **tsiy**-tun(g)*
page	**die Seite** *dee **ziy**-te(r)*

to paint	**malen** *mah-le(r)n*
paper	**das Papier** *das pa-peer*
pen	**der Kugelschreiber** *dair koo-ge(r)l-shriy-be(r)*
pencil	**der Bleistift** *dair bliy-shtift*
pencil sharpener	**der Spitzer** *dair shpit-tser*
picture	**das Bild** *das bilt*
poem	**das Gedicht** *das ge(r)-dikht*
question mark	**das Fragezeichen** *das frah-ge(r)-tsiy-khe(r)n*
to read	**lesen** *lay-ze(r)n*
rubber	**der Gummi** *dair gu-mee*
ruler	**das Lineal** *das li-ne-ahl*
sentence	**der Satz** *dair zats*
story	**die Geschichte** *dee ge(r)-shikh-te(r)*
to spell	**buchstabieren** *bookh-shta-beer-e(r)n*
spelling	**die Rechtschreibung** *dee rekht-shriy-bun(g)*
word	**das Wort** *das vort*
to write	**schreiben** *shriy-be(r)n*

toys, games and pastimes

board game	das Brettspiel
	*das **bret**-shpeel*
camera	die Kamera
	*dee **ka**-me-ra*
cassette, tape	die Kassette
	*dee ka-**se**-te(r)*
chess	das Schach
	das shakh
to collect	sammeln
	***za**-me(r)ln*
compact disc	die Compact Disc
	dee kom-pakt disk
computer	der Computer
	*dair kom-**pyoo**-ter*
to dance	tanzen
	***tan**-tse(r)n*
dice	der Würfel
	*dair **v(y)oor**-fe(r)l*
doll	die Puppe
	*dee **pu**-pe(r)*
doll's house	das Puppenhaus
	*das **pu**-pe(r)n-hows*
fishing	das Angeln
	*das **an(g)**-e(r)ln*
game	das Spiel
	das shpeel
hide-and-seek	das Versteckspiel
	*das fair-**shtek**-shpeel*
hobby	das Hobby
	*das **ho**-bee*
hopscotch	das Himmel-und-Hölle-Spiel
	*das hi-me(r)l-unt-**huh**-le(r)-shpeel*

jigsaw	das Puzzle *das **pa**-zl*
leap-frog	das Bockspringen *das **bok**-shprin(g)-e(r)n*
model	das Modell *das mo-**del***
photo	das Photo *das **foh**-toh*
to play	spielen ***shpee**-le(r)n*
playing card	die Spielkarte *dee **shpeel**-kar-te(r)*
radio	das Radio *das **rah**-di-oh*
record	die Platte *dee **pla**-te(r)*
roller skate	der Rollschuh *dair **rol**-shoo*
skateboard	das Skateboard *das **skayt**-bord*
stamp	die Briefmarke *dee **breef**-mar-ke(r)*
stereo	die Stereoanlage *dee **shtay**-ray-oh-an-lah-ge(r)*
teddy bear	der Teddy *dair **te**-dee*
toy	das Spielzeug *das **shpeel**-tsoyg*
toy soldier	der Spielzeugsoldat *dair **shpeel**-tsoyg-zol-daht*
train set	die Spielzeugeisenbahn *dee **shpeel**-tsoyg-iy-ze(r)n-bahn*

sport

athletics	die Leichtathletik
	dee liykht-at-lay-teek

ball	der Ball
	dair bal

cricket	das Kricket
	das kri-ket

football	der Fussball
	dair foos-bal

football boot	der Fussballschuh
	dair foos-bal-shoo

football match	das Fussballspiel
	das foos-bal-shpeel

to lose	verlieren
	fair-leer-e(r)n

snooker	das Snooker
	das snoo-ker

sport	der Sport
	dair shport

to swim	schwimmen
	shvi-me(r)n

swimming	das Schwimmen
	das shvi-me(r)n

swimming costume	der Badeanzug
	dair bah-de(r)-an-tsoog

swimming pool	das Schwimmbad
	das shvim-baht

table tennis	das Tischtennis
	das tish-te-nis

tennis	das Tennis
	das te-nis

tracksuit	der Traininganzug
	dair tray-nin(g)-an-tsoog

to win	gewinnen
	ge(r)-vi-ne(r)n

music and singing

choir   der Chor
*dair **koh**-er*

drum   die Trommel
*dee **tro**-me(r)l*

guitar   die Gitarre
*dee gi-**ta**-re(r)*

hymn   die Hymne
*dee **h(y)um**-ne(r)*

instrument   das Instrument
*das in-stroo-**ment***

orchestra   das Orchester
*das or-**kes**-ter*

organ   die Orgel
*dee **or**-ge(r)l*

piano   das Klavier
*das kla-**veer***

pop music   die Popmusik
*dee **pop**-moo-zeek*

recorder   die Blockflöte
*dee **blok**-fluhte(r)*

to sing   singen
***zin(g)**-e(r)n*

singer   der Sänger, die Sängerin
*dair **zen(g)**-e(r), dee **zen(g)**-e(r)-rin*

song   das Lied
das leet

trumpet   die Trompete
*dee trom-**pay**-te(r)*

tune   die Melodie
*dee me-lo-**dee***

violin   die Geige
*dee **giy**-ge(r)*

voice   die Stimme
*dee **sti**-me(r)*

television

advert	der Werbespot
	*dair **vair**-be(r)-spot*
aerial	die Antenne
	*dee an-**te**-ne(r)*
cartoon	der Trickfilm
	*dair **trik**-film*
channel	der Kanal
	*dair ka-**nahl***
comedy	die Komödie
	*dee ko-**muh**-dee-e(r)*
film	der Film
	dair film
news	die Nachrichten
	*dee **nakh**-rikh-ten*
programme	die Sendung
	*dee **zen**-dun(g)*
quiz	das Quiz
	das kvis
remote control	die Fernkontrolle
	*dee **fairn**-kon-tro-le(r)*
screen	der Schirm
	dair sheerm
television	das Fernsehen
	*das **fairn**-zay-e(r)n*
to turn off	ab'schalten
	***ap**-shal-te(r)n*
to turn on	ein'schalten
	***iyn**-shal-te(r)n*
video recorder	der Videorecorder
	*dair **vee**-day-oh-re-kor-der*
video tape	die Videocassette
	*dee **vee**-day-oh-ka-se-te(r)*
to watch	sich an'sehen
	*zikh **an**-zay-en*

making things

to build	bauen *bow*-e(r)n
cardboard	die Pappe *dee **pa**-pe(r)*
glass	das Glas *das glahs*
glue	der Klebstoff *dair **klayp**-shtof*
hammer	der Hammer *dair **ha**-mer*
to knit	stricken ***shtri**-ke(r)n*
metal	das Metall *das me-**tal***
nail	der Nagel *dair **nah**-ge(r)l*
needle	die Nadel *dee **nah**-de(r)l*
plastic	das Plastik *das **plas**-tik*
saw	die Säge *dee **zay**-ge(r)*
scissors	die Schere *dee **shair**-e(r)*
to sew	nähen ***nay**-e(r)n*
to stick	kleben ***klay**-be(r)n*
string	die Schnur *dee shnoor*
wood	das Holz *das holts*
wool	die Wolle *dee **vo**-le(r)*

containers

bag	die Tasche *dee **ta**-she(r)*
bottle	die Flasche *dee **fla**-she(r)*
box	die Kiste *dee **kis**-te(r)*
bucket	der Eimer *dair **iy**-mer*
cage	der Käfig *dair **kay**-fig*
drawer	die Schublade *dee **shoop**-lah-de(r)*
handbag	die Handtasche *dee **hant**-ta-she(r)*
jar	das Glas *das glahs*
jug	der Krug *dair kroog*
kettle	der Kessel *dair **ke**-se(r)l*
packet	das Paket *das pa-**kayt***
pocket	die Tasche *dee **ta**-she(r)*
purse	das Portemonnaie *das port-mo-**nay***
suitcase	der Koffer *dair **ko**-fe(r)*
teapot	die Teekanne *dee **tay**-ka-ne(r)*
tin	die Dose *dee **doh**-ze(r)*
wallet	die Brieftasche *dee **breef**-ta-she(r)*

animals

animal	das Tier *das teer*
bear	der Bär *dair bayr*
bull	der Stier *dair shteer*
camel	das Kamel *das ka-**mel***
cat	die Katze *dee **kat**-tse*
cow	die Kuh *dee koo*
dog	der Hund *dair hunt*
donkey	der Esel *dair **ay**-ze(r)l*
elephant	der Elefant *dair e-le-**fant***
fish	der Fisch *dair fish*
fox	der Fuchs *dair fuks*
frog	der Frosch *dair frosh*
giraffe	die Giraffe *dee gi-**ra**-fe(r)*
goldfish	der Goldfisch *dair **golt**-fish*
gorilla	der Gorilla *dair go-**ri**-la*
guinea pig	das Meerschweinchen *das **mayr**-shwiyn-she(r)n*
hamster	der Hamster *dair **ham**-ster*

horse	**das Pferd** *das pfairt*
kitten	**das Kätzchen** *das **kets**-she(r)n*
lamb	**das Lamm** *das lam*
lion	**der Löwe** *dair **luh**-ve(r)*
monkey	**der Affe** *dair **a**-fe(r)*
mouse	**die Maus** *dee mows*
pig	**das Schwein** *das shwiyn*
puppy	**das Hundchen** *das **hunt**-she(r)n*
rabbit	**das Kaninchen** *das ka-**neen**-she(r)n*
rat	**die Ratte** *dee **ra**-te(r)*
rhinoceros	**das Rhinozeros** *das ri-**noh**-tse-ros*
sheep	**das Schaf** *das shahf*
snake	**die Schlange** *dee **shlan(g)**-e(r)*
tiger	**der Tiger** *dair **tee**-ger*
tortoise	**die Schildkröte** *dee **shilt**-kruh-te(r)*
turtle	**die Wasserschildkröte** *dee **va**-ser-shilt-kruh-te(r)*
zebra	**das Zebra** *das **tsay**-bra*

birds, insects and small creatures

ant
die Ameise
*dee **ah**-miy-ze(r)*

bee
die Biene
*dee **bee**-ne(r)*

bird
der Vogel
*dair **foh**-ge(r)l*

butterfly
der Schmetterling
*dair **shme**-ter-lin(g)*

duck
die Ente
*dee **en**-te(r)*

eagle
der Adler
*dair **ahd**-ler*

fly
die Fliege
*dee **flee**-ge(r)*

hen
das Huhn
das hoon

moth
der Nachtfalter
*dair **nakht**-fal-ter*

parrot
der Papagei
*dair pa-pa-**giy***

pigeon
die Taube
*dee **tow**-be(r)*

snail
die Schnecke
*dee **shne**-ke(r)*

sparrow
der Sperling
*dair **shpair**-lin(g)*

spider
die Spinne
*dee **shpi**-ne(r)*

swan
der Schwan
dair shvahn

wasp
die Wespe
*dee **ves**-pe(r)*

places

airport	der Flughafen *dair floog-hah-fe(r)n*
beach	der Strand *dair shtrant*
city	die Grossstadt *dee grohs-shtat*
continent	der Kontinent *dair kon-ti-nent*
country	das Land *das lant*
countryside	das Land *das lant*
desert	die Wüste *dee v(y)oos-te(r)*
farm	der Bauernhof *dair bow-ern-hohf*
field	das Feld *das felt*
jungle	der Dschungel *dair chun(g)-e(r)l*
mountain	der Berg *dair bairg*
park	das Park *das park*
road	die Strasse *dee shtrah-se(r)*
station	der Bahnhof *dair bahn-hohf*
street	die Strasse *dee shtrah-se(r)*
town	die Stadt *dee shtat*
village	das Dorf *das dorf*

countries and continents

Africa   Afrika (n)
ah-fri-ka

America   Amerika (n)
a-may-ri-ka

Argentina   Argentinien (n)
ar-gen-tee-nee-e(r)n

Asia   Asien (n)
ah-zee-e(r)n

Australia   Australien (n)
ows-trah-lee-e(r)n

Austria   Österreich (n)
uhs-ter-riykh

Belgium   Belgien (n)
bel-gee-e(r)n

Brazil   Brasilien (n)
bra-zee-lee-e(r)n

Britain   Grossbritannien (n)
grohs-bri-ta-nee-e(r)n

Canada   Kanada (n)
ka-na-da

China   China (n)
khee-na

England   England (n)
en(g)-lant

Europe   Europa (n)
oy-roh-pa

France   Frankreich (n)
frank-riykh

Germany   Deutschland (n)
doytsh-lant

Greece   Griechenland (n)
gree-khe(r)n-lant

Holland   Holland (n)
ho-lant

India	Indien (n)
	in-dee-e(r)n
Ireland	Irland (n)
	eer-lant
Italy	Italien (n)
	i-tah-lee-e(r)n
Japan	Japan (n)
	yah-pan
New Zealand	Neuseeland (n)
	noy-zay-lant
Pakistan	Pakistan (n)
	pah-kis-tan
Portugal	Portugal (n)
	por-tu-gal
Russia	Russland (n)
	rus-lant
Scotland	Schottland (n)
	shot-lant
South Africa	Südafrika (n)
	z(y)ood-ah-fri-ka
Spain	Spanien (n)
	spah-nee-e(r)n
Switzerland	die Schweiz
	dee shviyts
U.S.A.	die Vereinigten Staaten
	dee fair-iy-nig-te(r)n shtah-te(r)n
Wales	Wales (n)
	waylz
West Indies	die Westindischen Inseln
	dee vest-in-di-she(r)n in-ze(r)ln

areas of water

canal	der Kanal *dair ka-**nahl***
lake	der See *dair zay*
ocean	der Ozean *dair **oh**-tse-an*
pond	der Teich *dair tiykh*
river	der Fluss *dair flus*
sea	das Meer *das mayr*
stream	der Bach *dair bakh*

buildings

block of flats	der Wohnblock *dair **vohn**-blok*
building	das Gebaüde *das ge(r)-**boy**-de(r)*
church	die Kirche *dee **keer**-khe(r)*
factory	die Fabrik *dee fa-**breek***
hospital	das Krankenhaus *das **kran(g)**-ke(r)n-hows*
hotel	das Hotel *das ho-**tel***
museum	das Museum *das mu-**zay**-um*
office	das Büro *das b(y)oo-**roh***

shopping

bank   **die Bank**
dee bank

to buy   **kaufen**
***kow**-fe(r)n*

change
(money)   **das Kleingeld**
*das **kliyn**-gelt*

chemist's   **die Apotheke**
*dee a-po-**tay**-ke(r)*

department store   **das Kaufhaus**
*das **kowf**-hows*

greengrocer's   **der Gemüseladen**
*dair ge(r)-**m(y)oo**-ze(r)-lah-de(r)n*

grocer's   **das Lebensmittelgeschäft**
*das **lay**-be(r)ns-mi-te(r)l-ge(r)-sheft*

market   **der Markt**
dair markt

money   **das Geld**
das gelt

newsagent's   **der Zeitungshändler**
*dair **tsiy**-tun(g)s-hend-ler*

pet shop   **die Tierhandlung**
*dee **teer**-hand-lun(g)*

post office   **das Postamt**
*das **post**-amt*

to sell   **verkaufen**
*fair-**kow**-fe(r)n*

shop   **das Geschäft**
*das ge(r)-**sheft***

to spend   **aus'geben**
***ows**-gay-be(r)n*

supermarket   **der Supermarkt**
*dair **zu**-per-markt*

toy shop   **der Spielwarenladen**
*dair **shpeel**-vah-re(r)n-lah-de(r)n*

people and their jobs

bus conductor — der Busschaffner
*dair **bus**-shaf-ner*

doctor — der Arzt, die Ärztin
*dair ahrtst, dee **airts**-tin*

driver — der Fahrer, die Fahrerin
*dair **fah**-rer, dee **fah**-re(r)-rin*

farmer — der Bauer
*dair **bow**-er*

fireman — der Feuerwehrmann
*dair **foy**-er-vair-man*

job — die Stelle
*dee **shte**-le(r)*

king — der König
*dair **kuh**-nig*

nurse — die Krankenschwester
*dee **kran(g)**-ke(r)n-shves-ter*

policeman — der Polizist
*dair po-li-**tsist***

policewoman — die Polizistin
*dee po-li-**tsist**-in*

postman — der briefträger
*dair **breef**-tray-ger*

queen — die Königin
*dee **kuh**-ni-gin*

shopkeeper — der Geschäftsinhaber
*dair ge(r)-**shefts**-in-hah-ber*

soldier — der Soldat
*dair zol-**daht***

vet — der Tierarzt, die Tierärztin
*dair **teer**-ahrtst, dee **teer**-airts-tin*

work — die Arbeit
*dee **ar**-biyt*

to work — arbeiten
***ar**-biy-te(r)n*

vehicles

aeroplane	das Flugzeug *das **floog**-tsoyg*
bicycle	das Fahrrad *das **fahr**-raht*
boat	das Boot *das boht*
bus	der Bus *dair bus*
car	das Auto *das **ow**-toh*
helicopter	der Hubschrauber *dair **hoop**-shrow-ber*
lorry	der Lkw *dair el-kah-vay*
motorbike	das Motorrad *das **moh**-tor-raht*
ship	das Schiff *das shif*
spaceship	das Raumschiff *das **rowm**-shif*
tank	der Panzer *dair **pan**-tser*
taxi	das Taxi *das **tak**-see*
tractor	der Traktor *dair **trak**-tor*
train	der Zug *dair tsoog*
van	der Lieferwagen *dair **lee**-fer-vah-ge(r)n*
vehicle	das Fahrzeug *das **fahr**-tsoyg*
wheel	das Rad *das raht*

moving, travelling and directions

to arrive	an'kommen *an*-ko-me(r)n
to drive	fahren *fah*-re(r)n
east	der Osten dair *os*-te(r)n
to fly	fliegen *flee*-ge(r)n
holiday	der Urlaub dair *oor*-lowp
journey	die Reise dee *riy*-ze(r)
to jump	springen *shprin(g)*-e(r)n
to leave	weg'gehen *vek*-gay-e(r)n
left	links *links*
north	der Norden dair *nor*-de(r)n
right	rechts *rekhts*
to ride *(a horse)*	reiten *riy*-te(r)n
to run	laufen *low*-fe(r)n
south	der Süden dair *z(y)oo*-de(r)n
to walk	zu Fuss gehen tsoo foos gay-e(r)n
west	der Westen dair *ves*-te(r)n

things you do with your head

to cough	husten *hoos-te(r)n*
to cry	weinen *viy-ne(r)n*
to hear	hören *huh-re(r)n*
to laugh	lachen *la-khe(r)n*
to listen	zu'hören *tsoo-huh-re(r)n*
to look	blicken *bli-ke(r)n*
to look at	an'sehen *an-zay-e(r)n*
to say, to tell	sagen *zah-ge(r)n*
to see	sehen *zay-e(r)n*
to shout	schreien *shriy-e(r)n*
to smell	riechen *ree-khe(r)n*
to smile	lächeln *le-khe(r)ln*
to sneeze	niesen *nee-ze(r)n*
to speak	sprechen *shpre-khe(r)n*
to taste	schmecken *shme-ke(r)n*
to think	denken *den(g)-ke(r)n*

things you do with your hands

to carry	tragen *trah*-ge(r)n
to catch	fangen *fan(g)*-e(r)n
to close	schliessen *shlee*-se(r)n
to lift	heben *hay*-be(r)n
to give	geben *gay*-be(r)n
to hit	schlagen *shlah*-ge(r)n
to hold	halten *hal*-te(r)n
to open	öffnen *uhf*-ne(r)n
to pick up	auf'heben *owf*-hay-be(r)n
to pull	ziehen *tsee*-e(r)n
to push	schieben *shee*-be(r)n
to put	stellen *shte*-le(r)n
to scratch	kratzen *kra*-tse(r)n
to take	nehmen *nay*-me(r)n
to throw	werfen *vair*-fe(r)n
to touch	berühren be(r)-*r(y)oor*-e(r)n

colours and shapes

black	schwarz *shvarts*
blue	blau *blow*
brown	braun *brown*
circle	der Kreis *dair kriys*
colour	die Farbe *dee **far**-be(r)*
green	grün *gr(y)oon*
grey	grau *grow*
orange	orange *oh-rah(n)-zhe(r)*
pink	rosa ***roh**-za*
purple	violett *vee-oh-**let***
rectangle	das Rechteck *das **rekht**-ek*
red	rot *roht*
shape	die Form *dee form*
square	das Quadrat *das kva-**draht***
triangle	das Dreieck *das **driy**-ek*
white	weiss *viys*
yellow	gelb *gelp*

describing people

angry	**zornig** *tsor*-nig
beautiful	**schön** *shuhn*
brave	**mutig** *moo*-tig
clever	**klug** *kloog*
dishonest	**unehrlich** *un*-air-likh
fat	**dick** *dik*
friendly	**freundlich** *froynt*-likh
he is handsome	**er sieht gut aus** *air zeet goot ows*
happy	**glücklich** *gl(y)uk*-likh
healthy	**gesund** *ge(r)-zunt*
honest	**ehrlich** *air*-likh
kind	**nett** *net*
naughty	**unartig** *un*-ar-tig
old	**alt** *alt*
polite	**höflich** *huhf*-likh
poor	**arm** *arm*
pretty	**hübsch** *h(y)oobsh*

rich	reich	*riykh*
rude	unhöflich	**un**-*huhf-likh*
sad	traurig	**trow**-*rig*
short	klein	*kliyn*
sick	krank	*krank*
slim	schlank	*shlank*
strong	stark	*shtark*
stupid	dumm	*dum*
tall	gross	*grohs*
tired	müde	**m(y)oo**-*de(r)*
ugly	hässlich	**hes**-*likh*
unfriendly	unfreundlich	**un**-*froynt-likh*
weak	schwach	*shvakh*
young	jung	*yun(g)*

describing things

bad	**schlecht** *shlekht*
big, large	**gross** *grohs*
bright	**hell** *hel*
cheap	**billig** ***bi**-lig*
dark	**dunkel** ***dun(g)**-ke(r)l*
deep	**tief** *teef*
difficult	**schwierig** ***shveer**-ig*
dry	**trocken** ***tro**-ke(r)n*
easy	**leicht** *liykht*
expensive	**teuer** ***toy**-er*
false	**falsch** *falsh*
flat	**flach** *flakh*
good	**gut** *goot*
hard	**hart** *hart*
heavy	**schwer** *shvair*
high	**hoch** *hohkh*
interesting	**interessant** *in-te-re-**sant***

light *(in weight)*	**leicht** *liykht*
long	**lang** *lan(g)*
low	**niedrig** **nee**-*drig*
narrow	**eng** *en(g)*
new	**neu** *noy*
old	**alt** *alt*
quick	**schnell** *shnell*
round	**rund** *runt*
short	**kurz** *koorts*
slow	**langsam** **lan(g)**-*zahm*
small, little	**klein** *kliyn*
soft	**weich** *viykh*
thick	**dick** *dik*
thin	**dünn** *d(y)un*
true	**wahr** *vahr*
wet	**nass** *nas*
wide	**breit** *briyt*

numbers

1	eins	*iyns*
2	zwei	*tsviy*
3	drei	*driy*
4	vier	*feer*
5	fünf	*f(y)unf*
6	sechs	*zeks*
7	sieben	***zee**-be(r)n*
8	acht	*akht*
9	neun	*noyn*
10	zehn	*tsayn*
11	elf	*elf*
12	zwölf	*tsvuhlf*
13	dreizehn	***driy**-tsayn*
14	vierzehn	***feer**-tsayn*
15	fünfzehn	***f(y)unf**-tsayn*
16	sechzehn	***zekh**-tsayn*
17	siebzehn	***zeep**-tsayn*

18	achtzehn
	akht-tsayn
19	neunzehn
	noyn-tsayn
20	zwanzig
	tsvan-tsig
21	einundzwanzig
	ein-unt-tsvan-tsig
22	zweiundzwanzig
	tsviy-unt-tsvan-tsig
23	dreiundzwanzig
	driy-unt-tsvan-tsig
30	dreissig
	driy-sig
31	einunddreissig
	ein-unt-driy-sig
32	zweiunddreissig
	tsviy-unt-driy-sig
40	vierzig
	feer-tsig
50	fünfzig
	f(y)unf-tsig
60	sechzig
	zekh-tsig
70	siebzig
	zeep-tsig
80	achtzig
	akht-tsig
90	neunzig
	noyn-tsig
100	hundert
	hun-dert
1,000	tausend
	tow-ze(r)nt

other number words

first	erste *airs-te(r)*
second	zweite *tsviy-te(r)*
third	dritte *dri-te(r)*
fourth	vierte *feer-te(r)*
fifth	fünfte *f(y)unf-te(r)*
once	einmal *iyn-mahl*
twice	zweimal *tsviy-mahl*
half	die Hälfte *dee helf-te(r)*
quarter	das Viertel *das feer-te(r)l*
to add	addieren *a-deer-e(r)n*
to count	zählen *tsay-le(r)n*
to divide	dividieren *di-vi-deer-e(r)n*
fraction	der Bruch *dair brukh*
to multiply	multiplizieren *mul-ti-pli-tseer-e(r)n*
number	die Zahl *dee tsahl*
to subtract	subtrahieren *zup-tra-heer-e(r)n*
sum	die Rechenaufgabe *dee re-khe(r)n-owf-gah-be(r)*

time

afternoon	der Nachmittag *dair **nakh**-mi-tahg*
calendar	der Kalender *der ka-**len**-der*
century	das Jahrhundert *das yahr-**hun**-dert*
clock	die Uhr *dee oor*
date	das Datum *das **dah**-tum*
dawn	der Tagesanbruch *dair **tah**-ge(r)s-an-brukh*
day	der Tag *dair tahg*
early	früh *fr(y)oo*
evening	der Abend *dair **ah**-be(r)nt*
hour	die Stunde *dee **shtun**-de(r)*
late	spät *shpayt*
leap year	das Schaltjahr *das **shalt**-yahr*
midday	der Mittag *dair **mi**-tahg*
midnight	die Mitternacht *dee **mi**-ter-nakht*
minute	die Minute *dee mi-**noo**-te(r)*
month	der Monat *dair **moh**-nat*
morning	der Morgen *dair **mor**-ge(r)n*

night	**die Nacht** *dee nakht*
second	**die Sekunde** *dee se-__kun__-de(r)*
soon	**bald** *balt*
time	**die Zeit** *dee tsiyt*
today	**heute** **__hoy__**-*te(r)*
tomorrow	**morgen** **__mor__**-*ge(r)n*
watch	**die Armbanduhr** *dee* **__arm__**-*bant-uhr*
week	**die Woche** *dee* **__vo__**-*khe(r)*
weekend	**das Wochenende** *das* **__vo__**-*khe(r)n-en-de(r)*
year	**das Jahr** *das yahr*
yesterday	**gestern** **__ges__**-*tern*

telling the time

nine o'clock	**neun Uhr** *noyn oor*
half past nine	**halb zehn** *halp tsayn*
quarter past nine	**Viertel nach neun** **__feer__**-*te(r)l nakh noyn*
quarter to nine	**Viertel vor neun** **__feer__**-*te(r)l for noyn*

57

days of the week

Monday	Montag (m) *mohn-tahg*
Tuesday	Dienstag (m) *deenz-tahg*
Wednesday	Mittwoch (m) *mit-vokh*
Thursday	Donnerstag (m) *do-ners-tahg*
Friday	Freitag (m) *friy-tahg*
Saturday	Samstag (m) *zams-tahg*
Sunday	Sonntag (m) *zon-tahg*

seasons and festivals

autumn	der Herbst *dair hairpst*
Christmas	das Weihnachten *das viy-nakh-te(r)n*
Easter	das Ostern *das ohs-tairn*
New Year's Day	der Neujahrstag *dair noy-yahrs-tahg*
season	die Jahreszeit *dee yah-re(r)s-tsiyt*
spring	der Frühling *dair fr(y)oo-lin(g)*
summer	der Sommer *dair zo-mer*
winter	der Winter *dair vin-ter*

months of the year

January	Januar (m) *ya-noo-ar*
February	Februar (m) *fay-broo-ar*
March	März (m) *mairts*
April	April (m) *a-pril*
May	Mai (m) *miy*
June	Juni (m) *yoo-nee*
July	Juli (m) *yoo-lee*
August	August (m) *ow-gust*
September	September (m) *zep-tem-ber*
October	Oktober (m) *ok-toh-ber*
November	November (m) *noh-vem-ber*
December	Dezember (m) *de-tsem-ber*

weather

cloud   die Wolke
*dee **vol**-ke(r)*

cloudy   bewölkt
*be(r)-**vuhlkt***

cold   kalt
kalt

fog, mist   der Nebel
*dair **nay**-be(r)l*

foggy   nebelig
***nay**-be(r)-lig*

to freeze   frieren
***freer**-e(r)n*

hot   heiss
hiyss

ice   das Eis
das iys

lightning   der Blitz
dair blits

rain   der Regen
*dair **ray**-ge(r)n*

to rain   regnen
***rayg**-ne(r)n*

rainy   regnerisch
***rayg**-ne(r)-rish*

shower   der Schauer
*dair **show**-er*

snow   der Schnee
dair shnay

to snow   schneien
***shniy**-e(r)n*

storm   das Gewitter
*das ge(r)-**vi**-ter*

sunny   sonnig
***zo**-nig*

sunshine	der Sonnenschein
	*dair **zo**-ne(r)n-shiyn*
thunder	der Donner
	*dair **do**-ner*
umbrella	der Regenschirm
	*dair **ray**-ge(r)n-sheerm*
warm	warm
	varm
weather	das Wetter
	*das **ve**-ter*
wind	der Wind
	dair vint
windy	windig
	***vin**-dig*

things in the sky

moon	der Mond
	dair mohnt
planet	der Planet
	*dair pla-**nayt***
sky	der Himmel
	*dair **hi**-me(r)l*
star	der Stern
	dair shtairn
sun	die Sonne
	*dee **zo**-ne(r)*

where is it?
where is it going?

above	über *(y)oo-ber*
along	entlang *ent-lan(g)*
behind	hinter *hin-ter*
between	zwischen *tsvi-she(r)n*
in	in *in*
in front of	vor *for*
into	in *in*
next to	neben *nay-be(r)n*
on *(a table, the floor)*	auf *owf*
on *(the wall)*	an *an*
out of	aus *ows*
outside	draussen *drow-se(r)n*
through	durch *doorkh*
to	zu *tsoo*
towards	auf...zu *owf...tsoo*
under	unter *un-ter*

questions and answers

answer

die Antwort
*dee **ant**-vort*

to answer

antworten
***ant**-vor-te(r)n*

to ask

fragen
***frah**-ge(r)n*

to ask a question

eine Frage stellen
***iy**-ne(r) **frah**-ge(r) **shte**-le(r)n*

how?

wie?
vee

how many?

wie viele?
*vee **fee**-le(r)*

how much?

wieviel?
*vee-**feel***

if, whether

ob
op

to know

wissen
***vi**-se(r)n*

what?

was?
vas

where?

wo?
voh

when?

wann?
van

which?

welcher? welche? welches?
***vel**-kher   **vel**-khe(r)   **vel**-khe(r)s*

who?

wer?
vair

whose?

wessen?
***ve**-se(r)nq*

why?

warum?
*va-**rum***

question

die Frage
*dee **frah**-ge(r)*

useful little words

also	**auch** *owkh*
and	**und** *unt*
because	**weil** *viyl*
but	**aber** ***ah**-ber*
for	**für** *f(y)oor*
goodbye	**auf Wiedersehen** *owf **vee**-der-zay e(r)n*
hello	**hallo** ***ha**-loh*
a lot of	**viel, viele** *feel, **fee**-le(r)*
no	**nein** *niyn*
not	**nicht** *nikht*
of	**von** *fon*
please	**bitte** ***bi**-te(r)*
thank you	**danke schön** ***dan(g)**-ke(r) shuhn*
very	**sehr** *zair*
with	**mit** *mit*
without	**ohne** ***oh**-ne(r)*
yes	**ja** *yah*